A Super Sleuth's Manual

Jillian Powell
Illustrations by Alex Wohlrab and Fausto Bianchi

Contents

OXFORD
UNIVERSITY PRESS

Inspector Textor
on the case!

Inspector Textor here, inviting all you budding super sleuths to help me solve my latest case. A priceless necklace has been stolen from the mansion of retired Hollywood superstar, Dame Gloria Glossop. The first question on everyone's lips is ... who dunnit? Are you ready to help me find the clues and crack the case?

Case notes

Date: 29th February
Time: 07:30am
Dame Glossop is distraught – the missing necklace is worth £1 million! Her carer and her nephew are comforting her.

The Super Sleuth Manual

To be a top detective you need genius, guts and ... a manual. This is my trusted guide to forensics: the scientific techniques that can be used to investigate crimes. I'll be referring to it throughout the case. If there are hairs, fibres, fingerprints or footprints at the crime scene, I'll find 'em - and find out what they mean.

A Super Sleuth's Manual

A SUPER SLEUTH'S MANUAL

Crime Scene Investigation Team

Forensic experts search for **evidence** that can be used in a trial. Each time they find an item of evidence, they must preserve it, tag it and log it for the crime scene record. They use special skills, including:

- Fingerprinting
- **Chemical analysis** of samples
- Hair and fibre analysis
- Toxicology (analysis of poisons)
- Handwriting analysis

Fast fact

'Forensic evidence' is used in a court of law.

Let's get to work! I record every step of an investigation in my notebook. To start with, I'll work out who the key witnesses are and make a sketch of the crime scene. I'll also **probe** the security arrangements that Dame Glossop had in place.

The Crime at Glossop Hall

What?
£1 million necklace – vanished!
Gift from an A-list admirer

When?
A stormy Sunday night in February
Dame Glossop was watching the Oscars on TV, with her nephew Harry
Her carer Elena was upstairs, asleep

Where?
Necklace was locked inside safe, in drawing room
Safe hidden behind a large painting

Security
Safe has secret code
CCTV cameras fitted inside and outside the house

Clues
Drawing-room window broken
Footprint left in flower bed outside window

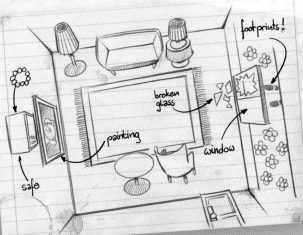

Being a distinguished detective of great experience, I'm starting to get a picture of what happened.

Witnesses ... or suspects?

Time for my favourite part of a case - interviewing the witnesses. Where was everyone at the time of the crime? Do they have an **alibi**? Even the smallest detail could be the clue that cracks the case. I record the interviews so they can be used as evidence. Look at my interview notes and **transcripts** carefully - who sounds most suspicious? Who would you interview again?

Dame Gloria Glossop, Retired filmstar (refuses to reveal her age)

- Lives on her own, except for her carer, Elena
- Keeps all her precious jewellery in a safe
- Keeps the code for the safe secret from everyone except her accountant, Mr Bevis
- Was watching television with nephew Harry at the time of the crime

"I don't know what I would do without Elena. She has only been with me a year but she is a friend as much as a carer. Mr Bevis? I gave him the code so he can access my accounts each week. It's important to keep on top of one's fortune! Bevis has been the family accountant for a decade. My husband trusted him like a friend."

Elena Smith, 25
Dame Glossop's live-in carer

— Has worked for Dame Glossop for a year and appears to be fond of her
— Loves her job, which allows her to support her elderly parents financially
— Says she was in her room asleep at the time of the crime
— Seems very upset by the crime

"Dame Glossop is a really nice employer. She is so kind. She is always lending her nephew money for something or other. But lately she has been a little forgetful and I do worry, as things go missing and we have to hunt for them."

Harry Glossop, 35
Dame Glossop's nephew

— Works in finance, dealing in stocks and shares
— Recently lost a lot of money
— Visits his aunt weekly
— Was watching television with Dame Glossop on the night of the crime

"We were watching the Oscars all night. Auntie never misses it - she knows most of the winners! Have you spoken to her accountant, Bevis? I don't trust the man. He takes way too much upon himself, thinking he's one of the family just because he knew my uncle."

Following up the leads

The first three interviews throw up some interesting **leads**. I ask Dame Glossop's accountant, Mr Bevis, to come to the house to be interviewed. I also interview Dame Glossop's **groundsman** and her cleaner when they turn up for work.

Tom Dodson, 38
Dame Glossop's groundsman

- Lives in a lodge on the Glossop estate
- Was out walking his dog at the time of the robbery and thinks he saw something

"I heard a rustling in the bushes and that was when I saw someone. They were creeping out of that window, quiet as anything. But when Eccles started barking, they ran like the clappers. I think they had something over their head because I couldn't see their face. They were wearing black, I remember that. They were slim, quite young, I would say."

Luka Brown, 26
Cleaner at Glossop Hall

- Has worked at the Hall for the last six months
- Was home alone on the night of the crime
- Very hard-working; almost started cleaning up the crime scene before I could stop him — which would have destroyed all the forensic evidence!

"I haven't seen the necklace before - only Elena is allowed to touch Dame Glossop's jewels, when she helps her get dressed. I was at home last night, yeah, watching the Oscars. No, I couldn't say who won, I fell asleep on the sofa. What a mess in the drawing room! Don't you want me to tidy up now?"

Bernard Bevis, 55
The Glossop family accountant, works at Bevis & Bevis

- Has worked for Dame Glossop since her husband died
- The only other person who knows the code to the safe
- Was working late at the time of the burglary

"Of course Dame Glossop trusted me with the safe code, I've worked for this family for ten years. I was at the office last night - you can call my daughter Lucy to check. Have you interviewed the nephew, Harry? He's always asking his aunt for money and she always gives in to him, against my advice. Her carer Elena is just as bad."

Case notes
I can't rule anyone out yet. Time to turn to my trusty *Super Sleuth Manual* and get to the bottom of this confusing crime.

Caught on camera

My initial investigations reveal that the house has CCTV security cameras. The first step is to watch the **footage** from the night of the crime. My *Super Sleuth's Manual* will tell me what to look out for ...

CCTV cameras

CCTV (Closed Circuit Television) is a network of cameras that are hooked up to a monitor system. The cameras view scenes that can be watched on screens as live or recorded action. Some cameras record action on to videotape. Others use digital video recording to a computer hard drive. Video footage can be viewed from anywhere via the Internet.

A CCTV camera

Scanning software

CCTV systems can scan traffic for car number plates. They can flag up suspicious behaviour or track suspects by recognizing their faces in a crowd. Some software is able to sort through 36 million faces a second to recognize and pick out a suspect's face. It can also flag up actions such as someone holding a gun, or track a criminal who returns frequently to the scene of a crime.

A CCTV circuit

Case study: pickpockets caught on CCTV

On 28th January 2014, British Transport Police arrested Claudiu-Viorel Stefan and his wife Andrea Sipos. The couple had been caught on camera months before, stealing from passengers on the London Underground. They left the country before they could be arrested.

They used the busy environment of the Underground to their advantage. They stood very close to passengers and then slipped their hands into their bags to steal items. The husband-and-wife team hadn't taken into account that they were being filmed by CCTV, as they stole from passengers. The pair were caught returning to the UK, thanks to similar cameras at Luton Airport. They were sentenced to 40 weeks in jail.

I've installed the very best system, you know, with the latest scanning software.

evidence log 1

Footage from Dame Glossop's CCTV camera.

evidence log 2

Enhancing images

Just as I thought! The intruder has been caught on camera! Slim and shadowy – this certainly matches Tom Dodson's witness statement. Let's zoom in for a closer look ...

Video forensic experts can use software to enhance images. Some software can magnify and refocus video recordings so powerfully that it can zoom in on someone's arm to measure their pulse. It does this by separating out each pixel from a video image and examining tiny changes in colour to detect the pulse under the skin.

Facial imaging

Even where they are not able to enhance footage, detectives may use facial imaging and call on body-language experts to find out if someone on CCTV matches their suspect. Facial-imaging experts can examine facial features, such as the space between the eyes or the length of the nose. They can also examine details of clothing, such as the logo on a T-shirt or a brand mark on trainers. Body-language experts look at the way someone stands or walks, and anything they do which might suggest they are tense, angry or nervous.

Imaging experts examine the dimensions and features of faces.

Video evidence

For video evidence to be used in court, it must have a **chain of custody**. This means no one could have edited or altered it. Video forensic experts examine evidence on camera recordings, smartphones and other media devices to check for signs that it has been edited. These signs could be sudden changes of scene or repetition of the same shot or frame.

Case notes

Zooming in reveals that the cunning criminal evaded Dame Glossop's expensive recognition software by disguising their face with a stocking! But it also reveals a number, written on the intruder's hand.

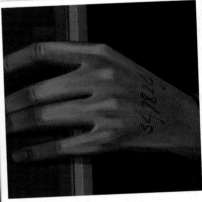

evidence log 3

"That's the code to my safe!"

"Well, that proves it wasn't me - I wouldn't have had to write the code down!"

Examining the scene

I've done all I can from a distance – time to plunge into the crime scene, to hunt for more clues. As many an expert in the field has said, all contact with a crime scene is traceable. Let's find out how the forensics experts find those traces ...

Examining the scene

For murder and other serious crimes, the forensics team is often the one that starts the investigation. This team retrieves and records as much evidence as possible from the scene of the crime. They wear protective clothing and gloves and use special equipment so they won't **contaminate** any **trace evidence**.

The first step, before they touch anything, is to carefully take photographs or videos or make sketches of the scene. Next, they will *very carefully* start collecting potential evidence. They will, for example, lift hairs off clothing using tweezers rather than their fingers. This means they don't disturb the fabric, which could contain other trace evidence, such as make-up.

Forensics examining a crime scene.

Fingerprinting

Fingerprints are valuable evidence because no two people's fingerprints are exactly the same. Fingertips are covered with minute ridges and patterns known as 'characteristics'. Dirt, sweat or oils on the skin collect in these ridges to leave a print behind.

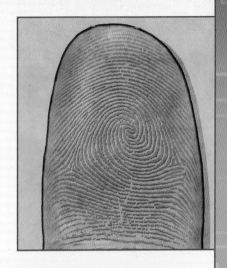

Case study: Henry classification system

In 1896, the commissioner of the Metropolitan Police in London, Sir Edward Henry, created a classification system for fingerprints. He added to the work of others who had discovered that fingerprints could be identified according to the different patterns they produced. In 1901, Sir Henry set up the Fingerprint Bureau at Scotland Yard. The following year, fingerprint evidence was used for the first time in an English court of law.

Fast fact

In 1910, the French professor, Edmond Locard, 'the Sherlock Holmes of France', set up the first police laboratory for forensic criminology.

Case notes
Next step: dust the crime scene for fingerprints, including key surfaces such as the windowsill and around the safe.

Fingerprint evidence

Forensic teams use several methods to reveal prints. Magnesium powder can be brushed on to surfaces; then the fingerprints can be photographed or lifted using tape. Other chemicals can be applied that release **vapours** which react with salts and oils in the print. Ultraviolet light can also be used to reveal fingerprints that are otherwise invisible.

Forensic team member dusting for fingerprints.

A Super Sleuth's Guide to ... Taking Fingerprints

1. Touch your face or hair with your fingertips, then touch a window pane.

2. Use a soft paintbrush to brush a light coat of cocoa powder on to the glass and blow away any surplus.

3. Carefully place a piece of sticky tape over the print, then peel it away.

4. Stick the tape down on to a plain piece of card to record your fingerprints. Do you have loops, whorls or arches?

Fast fact

There are three main types of characteristics: loops, whorls and arches.

Loop   Whorl   Arch

Watch where you put that powder. Those are priceless antiques, you know!

High-resolution prints

Forensic scientists in China have developed a new method for creating **high-resolution** fingerprints. Prints are transferred to a metallic plate and then coated in a chemical solution. The oily matter in the fingerprints repels the chemicals. Forensic scientists can then use an electrical charge to create a detailed 'negative' of the print.

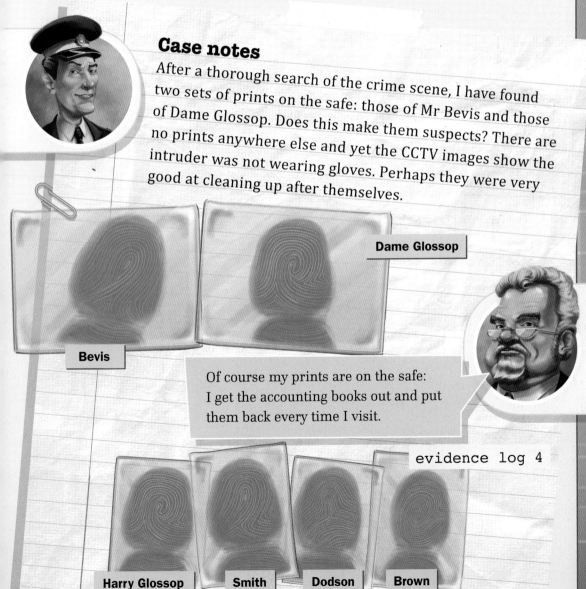

Case notes

After a thorough search of the crime scene, I have found two sets of prints on the safe: those of Mr Bevis and those of Dame Glossop. Does this make them suspects? There are no prints anywhere else and yet the CCTV images show the intruder was not wearing gloves. Perhaps they were very good at cleaning up after themselves.

Dame Glossop

Bevis

Of course my prints are on the safe: I get the accounting books out and put them back every time I visit.

evidence log 4

Harry Glossop   Smith   Dodson   Brown

Footprints

In my initial search of the crime scene, I found a footprint in the rose border outside the window where the intruder entered Glossop Hall. Let's find out what it can tell me.

evidence log 5

Examining footprints

Footprints left at a crime scene can be studied, recorded and matched to prints found at other locations. Criminals can leave three-dimensional (**3-D**) prints when they step on to soft ground, sand or snow. Two-dimensional (**2-D**) prints may also be left where soiled shoes have trodden dirt or other materials on to another surface, such as a carpet.

Photographs and casting

To preserve footprints as evidence, forensic teams take photographs that can be scanned into computers for analysis. They can dust footprints on flat surfaces with a fine powder, or use chemicals or dyes to make the prints easier to see. Sometimes footprints leave 3-D impressions. Casts of these prints can sometimes be made by pouring a casting mix into the imprint and allowing it to set. The cast can then be removed in one piece, making an exact replica of the print.

A crime scene officer taking an impression of a foot print.

A Super Sleuth's Guide to ...
Casting Footprints

1. Ask people wearing different types of shoes or trainers to step firmly on to soft ground or snow.

2. Use a large paintbrush to brush any loose dirt or soil away from the prints.

3. Add water to some plaster of Paris to make a soft paste. Carefully pour the paste into each print, smooth it down and wait for it to set.

4. When it has set, use a stick to prise up the cast. Brush away any dirt or loose matter.

5. Try matching the casts to the soles of the people's shoes or trainers to identify who made the print.

Case notes

I have taken a cast of the 3-D print in the rose border to identify the type and size of shoe the intruder was wearing. Help me crossmatch it against the shoes of our witnesses.

evidence log 6

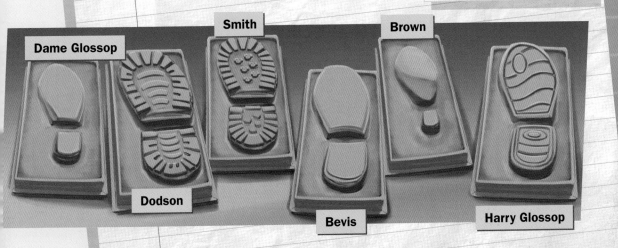

Dame Glossop

Smith

Brown

Dodson

Bevis

Harry Glossop

The intruder stepped in mud outside the window but there are no traces of mud inside. They must have left the boots in the rose border. However, I have found faint, sticky 2-D sock prints on the drawing-room floor.

Footprint data

Footprints can provide useful information about suspects at crime scenes. Forensic experts examine the soles to discover the size and brand of shoe a suspect was wearing. They can use the measurements of a footprint to work out a suspect's height and weight and even how fast they were walking or running. They do this by analysing data such as the depth of the print, how hard the ground was and whether it was dry or damp at the time the print was made.

A forensic expert collecting footprint evidence.

Shoe prints are also examined for wear marks or scratches. Wear patterns can give telltale clues about the wearer. For example, if they roll their foot inwards as they walk there will be more wear on the inside of the sole, which shows up on the print.

Footwear database

New software can be used to compare shoe prints, or even parts of print, found at crime scenes against a **database**. The software breaks down sole patterns into lines, circles and other shapes in the same way that fingerprints are analysed by their characteristics.

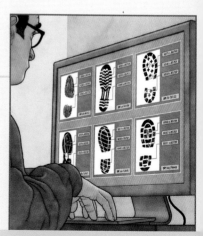

Analysing shoe prints against an online database.

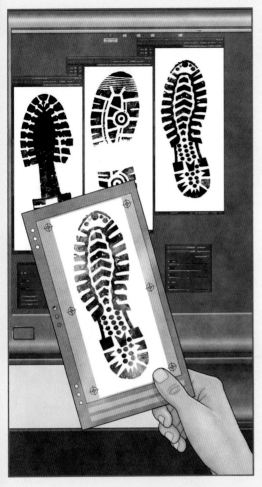

A Super Sleuth's Guide to ... Examining 2-D Footprints

1. Choose a shoe or trainer with an interesting sole pattern and make a rubbing of it using tracing paper and a wax crayon.

2. Measure and label the length and width, and label anything interesting, such as a brand mark in the sole design, or obvious wear marks.

Fast fact

The length of a person's foot is approximately 15 per cent of their height.

Case notes

The footprint outside the window matches the sole of Elena's size 7 wellington boot. But analysis of the sticky sock prints left in the drawing room suggests that the intruder has size 5 feet. This raises a question: why was the intruder too small for their boots? And there's another question: what is the mystery substance that was stuck to their socks?

Analytical chemistry

I suspect the footprint in the rose border is a **red herring,** planted to throw me off the scent. It would have worked – but the intruder's socks were coated with a sticky substance that has left footprints all over the drawing-room floor! I have collected samples carefully to avoid contamination and have sent them for analysis.

Forensic chemists analyse different substances. They can identify what they are and match them against other samples from different sources. They use a range of methods to do this. They test samples for chemical reactions in test tubes and they examine tiny particles under microscopes. They can even separate out substances using **solvents** or gases.

Forensic officers search for tiny particles that will form evidence.

Microchemistry

To examine the tiniest of samples – scientists use microchemistry. Sometimes these samples are less than a milligram in mass or a millilitre in volume. Scientists collect samples using **swab** kits and examine them under powerful scanning electron microscopes.

A scientist examining samples.

Separating compounds

Some samples can be identified by separating them into their different chemical parts. Gases such as helium and hydrogen can be used to separate substances. This is called gas **chromatography**. First, a machine heats a sample until it turns into a vapour. The vapour is then passed through the helium or hydrogen gas. This separates it out into its different **components**. A special electronic machine is used to identify the component parts of the sample and record them as peaks on a chart. These peaks can be used to identify and match the substance against other samples.

Case study: testing for poison

In 1836, a Scottish chemist, James Marsh, developed a chemical test to detect the poison arsenic. The test was used in 1840 to help solve the murder of Charles LaFarge, a French foundry-owner. The test was carried out on his dead body and confirmed that he had been poisoned with arsenic. LaFarge's wife, Marie, was suspected of the crime as she had recently bought the poison to kill rats. Thanks to the Marsh test, Marie was found guilty and sentenced to life in prison.

Case notes

The lab results are in and the mystery substance that coated the intruder's feet is ... floor polish! But where is it from?

Chromatography

Coloured chemical compounds can be separated out and identified using chromatography. In this process, the sample is placed on chromatography paper where it reacts with water or another solvent. As the paper soaks up the solvent, the sample separates out into its different components, creating different patterns and colours. These patterns identify the compound and can be compared to and matched with those from other samples.

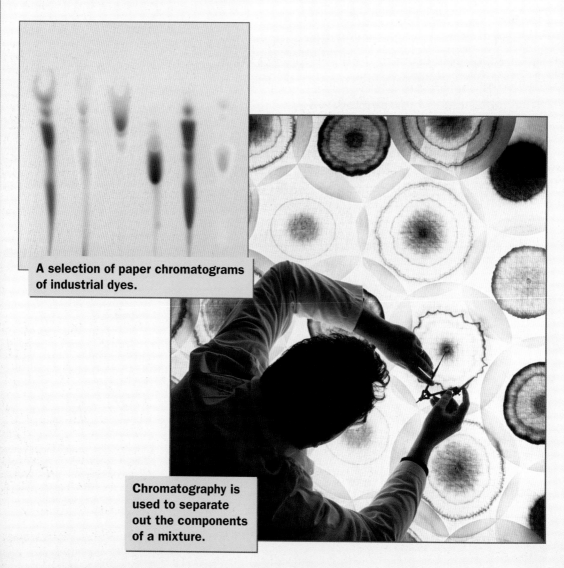

A selection of paper chromatograms of industrial dyes.

Chromatography is used to separate out the components of a mixture.

A Super Sleuth's Guide to ... Chromatography

This simple chromatography experiment will help super sleuths to identify different inks.

1. Cut a paper towel into 2.5 cm-wide strips.
2. Draw horizontal lines about 2.5 cm from the bottom of each strip using five different brands of black marker pen. Label each strip to identify which pen was used.

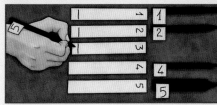

3. Hang the strips over a bowl of water so that the bottom of each one is just touching the water. As the water creeps up the strips, the black inks will separate into different colours and patterns.

4. Ask a friend to draw another line on a thin strip of paper using one of the pens, and repeat the experiment. Can you match the patterns from the first experiment and the second to identify which pen was used?

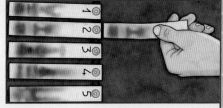

Case notes

I have been able to identify the brand of floor polish using chromatography. It's 'Gloss-up', the same floor polish used to make Dame Glossop's **parquet** hallway sparkle. The CCTV footage shows that the intruder did not leave the drawing room – so they must have been in the hallway on a different occasion. They must live or work in the house!

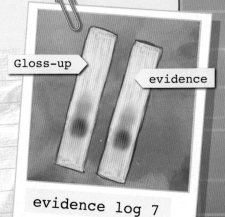

Gloss-up

evidence

evidence log 7

25

Trace evidence

The intruder was not very good at cleaning up after themselves. I have found more trace evidence at the crime scene: a hair on the drawing-room rug and a clothing fibre caught on a rose bush outside the window. These could be vital clues, so it's back to my *Super Sleuth's Manual* to find out what I need to do.

To collect trace evidence, forensic teams use special tweezers and magnifying lenses. Wearing protective gloves, they collect samples in tubes and bags that they seal immediately to prevent contamination. Smaller samples are lifted using special tape. The team can also use forensic **vacuums** with filters, which suck up samples onto paper for analysis in the laboratory. Hair and fibre samples can be examined to draw up a list of suspects and also to rule people out.

A forensic expert uses tweezers to collect trace evidence.

Hair analysis

Hair samples can be examined under microscopes or analysed using chemicals. Forensic scientists can tell from a hair sample if someone is male or female, and even their ethnic background.

Examining hair samples under the microscope can identify if hair found at the scene of a crime comes from one person or more.

A Super Sleuth's Guide to ... Analysing Hair Samples

1. Take one or more hairs from a comb or hairbrush and place in a plastic zip bag.

2. Examine the hair using a magnifying glass or microscope. To examine a hair using a microscope, first make a wet mount by putting a drop of water on the microscope slide. Carefully place the hair on top and examine it for characteristics. Look at colour, thickness, and whether it is coarse or smooth, dull or glossy, curly or straight.

3. Repeat with a different sample and record the differences.

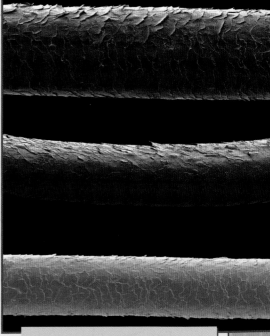

These hair samples come from people from three different ethnic backgrounds.

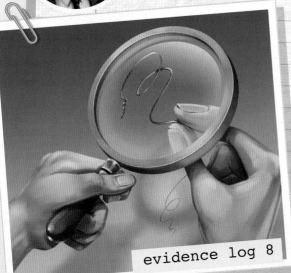

evidence log 8

Case notes

A careful look at the hair found at the scene reveals that it's long, curly and red. That seems to rule all the witnesses out. Perhaps the next section in my *Super Sleuth's Manual* will reveal more ...

DNA analysis

Forensic scientists can analyse DNA samples from hair, saliva and other body cells. Every person, except for identical twins, has different DNA. This is called their 'genetic code'. It makes everyone unique. This makes DNA analysis a reliable means of identification.

Fast fact

The human body has around 100 trillion cells and each one (apart from red blood cells) contains roughly two metres of DNA!

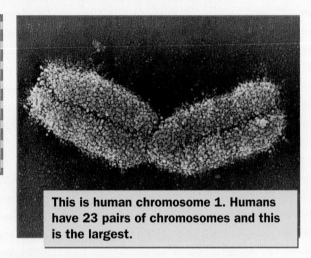

This is human chromosome 1. Humans have 23 pairs of chromosomes and this is the largest.

The results are back. DNA analysis confirms this hair is not an exact match to any of our witnesses. So who *does* it belong to?

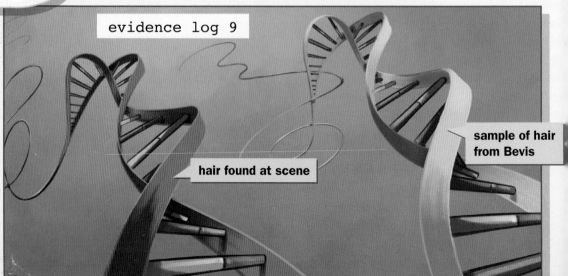

evidence log 9

hair found at scene

sample of hair from Bevis

Examining fibres

One method scientists use to identify samples of materials is to send infrared rays through them. By recording the amounts of radiation the materials absorb, they can analyse their structure and chemical make-up. They can sometimes identify the type of garment the sample comes from and even the brand.

A forensics officer lifting a sample of evidence using tape.

Lasers

Scientists can also use lasers to make molecules in a sample of material vibrate. As they vibrate, the molecules send out light rays of a different frequency from the light rays going in. Scientists can read the change in light frequency to identify different materials.

Case notes
Analysis of the fibre from the rose bush shows that it's cotton from a very expensive **pinstripe** suit. I'm so close to solving the crime but there's still one thing that's puzzling me. I'll sleep on it.

evidence log 10

Analysing handwriting

I was just drifting off to sleep when I had a thought. Perhaps the number written on the intruder's hand is the clue that could crack the case! My *Super Sleuth's Manual* has the know-how I need ...

Experts in handwriting analysis can help to solve crimes by identifying the writers of ransom notes, letters and other documents, such as wills. They can detect when someone has tried to disguise their handwriting and can identify forgeries.

No two people write in exactly the same way. A handwriting expert looks for characteristics including:

- Unusual slants or angles
- The way 't's are crossed and 'i's are dotted
- Unusual curls or loops
- Slants to left or right
- Average space between words and letters

Computer software can also be used to compare and match handwriting samples by creating 'statistical snapshots' of each letter and digit.

A forensic handwriting expert compares two handwriting samples side by side.

The way 't's are crossed and 'i's are dotted

Average space between words and letters

Unusual slants or angles

Can a room really be stolen? Yes – if you st...

In 1941, during World War II, Germany invaded...

...were under order to steal one of Russia's most...

...ous – the worldfamous Amber Room. So the Russian authorities tried to hide the room by camouflaging the amber walls with thin wallpaper. But it didn't work. It took fewer than two days for the German soldiers to strip the amber panels off the walls and pack them into crates. The 27 crates were taken to a castle in the German city of Königsberg.

What happened to it next is a mystery – the Amber Room has not been seen for over 60 years.

Unusual curls or loops

Slants to left or right

Case notes

The safe code was written on the back of the intruder's left hand. But they wore a watch on their right wrist, which suggests that they are left-handed. Someone else must have written the code on their left hand – they had an accomplice. Will the accomplice's handwriting give them away?

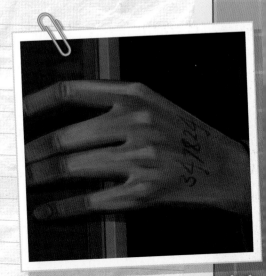

Invisible handwriting

A new day, and time to see if my hunch was right. The first step is to collect samples of handwriting from all our witnesses ...

Forensic document experts use special equipment to help them examine written documents. Filters and ultraviolet or infrared lights can be used to detect handwriting that is otherwise invisible. They can reveal where writing has been erased or show up faded writing. Sometimes, experts are able to tell where handwriting has been added in, using a different ink from the rest of a document or written on a different type of paper.

Case study: Joseph Cosey, master forger

In 1929, Joseph Cosey began a career in high-profile forgery. He forged signatures and letters of some of the most famous figures from US history, including President Abraham Lincoln and the writer Mark Twain. Cosey used special paper and inks to make careful forgeries that fooled many experts. He was very successful until, in 1937, he tried to sell a letter he said was written by President Lincoln. The dealer analysed the letter and found that it was a fake. Cosey was arrested and sentenced to three years in prison.

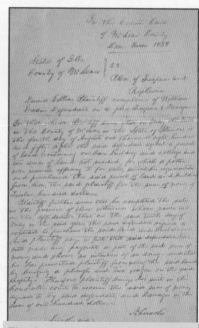

The forgery by Joseph Cosey of a document supposedly signed by Abraham Lincoln.

A Super Sleuth's Guide to ... Handwriting Analysis

1. Collect two or three handwritten signatures on separate pieces of thin white paper.

2. Take each piece of paper and fold a flap of paper over the signature. You can still see the signature through the flap.

3. On the flap, use a pen to make a dot at the top of each letter. Then connect the dots.

4. Now make a dot at the bottom of each letter and connect these dots. The dots at the top and bottom of the letters are the 'pattern' of the person's signature, which will remain the same even if the name is signed in a different way. Such patterns can help identify forgeries.

Case notes

This is the final piece of evidence. Do you know who committed the crime now? I have a pretty good idea.

FRIDAY 17th – DOGS TO VETS

£480
£472

24th July – Summer party

bread (3 loaves)
loose leaf tea (400g)
cheese for dinner party (7 varieties)

CCTV close-up of the code.

Invest £800 000 in....

Ring Sam – 549732

Reviewing the facts

It's time to review the evidence and see what I've discovered.

The facts

1. The CCTV footage shows an intruder breaking the window, entering the drawing-room, crossing the room to the safe and leaving through the window. Their face is disguised.

2. The only fingerprints found in the room are those of Dame Glossop and Mr Bevis, who both have access to the safe.

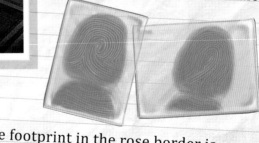

3. The footprint in the rose border is shown to be from a size 7 wellington boot. The burglar left the boots outside and entered the room in socks. Faint sock prints left inside the room show that the intruder has size 5 feet.

4. Chromatography reveals that the intruder had floor polish from the hallway on their socks. This definitely points the finger at someone who lives or works in the house.

5. The fibre caught on the rose bush is from a pinstripe suit but the CCTV footage shows the burglar dressed in black.

6. The hair found on the rug is long, curly and red. It doesn't match any of the samples taken from the witnesses. But analysis shows an interesting DNA match ...

7. CCTV footage reveals that the code for Dame Glossop's safe was written on the back of the intruder's left hand. The intruder is wearing a watch on their right hand, suggesting they are left-handed. I can deduce that someone else wrote the code down – the intruder had an accomplice. The writing has been analysed and compared with writing samples provided by suspects, to find a match.

Who dunnit?

My first impressions of the crime scene told me a story that pointed to Elena; but the forensic evidence told another. It's time to reveal what really happened ...

The intruder wore wellington boots to cross the muddy border - the same wellington boots worn by Elena!

The intruder smashed the window and climbed in, leaving the boots outside.

They opened the safe using a code written on their hand.

They were caught on CCTV - because they wanted to be!

The safe was empty. But the intruder knew this already!

They left empty-handed – leaving behind a trail of almost invisible sock prints and a single hair.

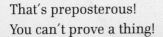

The next morning, Dame Glossop found the empty safe. The messy room and broken window all indicated the necklace had been taken that night. In fact, it had been taken out of the safe days before ... by someone who had the code, was allowed to use it, and had an alibi for that night. Mr Bevis!

They fled the scene, helped by an accomplice, who snagged their pinstripe suit on a rose bush.

That's preposterous! You can't prove a thing!

I can prove that the handwriting on the burglar's hand was yours and that it was a fibre from your suit caught on the rose bush. But one last question remains: who did you help climb out of the drawing-room window? Whose hand did you write the code on? Who was supposed to plant enough evidence to frame Elena ... but accidentally left some of her own? I can reveal that it was ...

... Luka, otherwise known as Lucy Bevis!

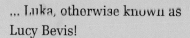

Dame Glossop, meet Mr Bevis's daughter – the other half of Bevis & Bevis. They were so worried that you were about to leave your fortune to Elena, they hatched a plan to frame her for the theft. Which is why the necklace was never taken out of Glossop Hall. You'll find it hidden in Elena's suitcase!

Another crime solved, thanks to my *Super Sleuth's Manual*. Thanks for your help with the forensic investigation. Now you're ready to start looking for clues of your own ...

Glossary

2-D having two dimensions; flat

3-D having three dimensions; having length, breadth and depth

alibi a claim that you cannot be guilty of a crime because you were somewhere else at the time

analysis an investigation of the parts that make up a whole

chain of custody a record of the location and movement movement and location of evidence from where it's obtained until used in court

chemical relating to the interaction of substances

chromatography a process that separates mixtures

component an individual part of something bigger

contaminate to pollute using an unwanted substance

database an organized collection of information on a computer

evidence information about a crime that is used in a court of law

footage a sequence forming part of a film or videotape

groundsman someone who looks after the grounds in a park or estate

high-resolution an image that is sharp and finely detailed

lead a clue pointing to a possible solution

parquet a type of patterned wooden floor

probe to question or examine closely

red herring a diversion intended to distract someone's attention

solvent a liquid that can dissolve other substances

swab a small piece of cotton used to obtain a specimen

trace evidence tiny pieces of evidence created when one object touches another

transcript a written or printed version of a sound recording

vacuum a device that collects dust and other particles by means of suction

vapour a chemical when it is in the form of a gas

Index

Supporting older children with reading

You can help your child to become a confident and enthusiastic reader by:

- finding a quiet time and place to read so they can read in comfort, without distractions
- creating a regular reading slot, such as before going to sleep, so reading becomes a habit
- talking about what they are reading and their reading likes and dislikes. This helps build their interest in what they are reading and develop personal choice in what they read.

Reading with your child

- Your child will read most of this book independently.
- You could still ask them to read a few pages to you. Be encouraging and positive – help them enjoy demonstrating their reading skills. As they read, encourage them to use expression in their voice to bring the text to life. This helps them become more fluent readers. If they do get stuck on a word encourage them to try to work it out. Check they understand the meaning of any new or difficult words.
- You could read a few pages to your child. This is particularly helpful if their interest seems to be flagging. Even older children still enjoy being read to. As well as increasing their interest and enjoyment, you are also showing that you too find reading something worth doing.

After reading this book

- Talk about what your child liked/disliked about this book.
- Reread the section on handwriting together. You could collect different handwriting samples from family and friends, and try to identify the different features.
- Ask your child to imagine that they are Inspector Textor interviewing the suspects about the robbery. You could be one of the suspects. Then you could swap roles.

Project X

Origins

Book Band 15
Dark Red

Oxford
Level 18

A Super Sleuth's Manual

On a stormy night in February, Dame Gloria Glossop's million-pound necklace was stolen. Take on the case and see if you can crack it.

Great for Guided Reading

Titles on the theme: *Who Dunnit?*

The Snatcher (Fiction)
Stolen Wonders (Fiction)
Mystery Cove (Fiction)
> **A Super Sleuth's Manual** (Non-fiction)
Unsolved Robberies (Non-fiction)

OXFORD
UNIVERSITY PRESS

How to get in touch:
web   www.oxfordprimary.co.uk
email primary.enquiries@oup.com
tel.   +44 (0) 1536 452610
fax   +44 (0) 1865 313472

ISBN 978-0-19-839411-2

9 780198 394112